THE
BELIEVER'S
SABBATH

Other Books by
JOHN G. REISINGER

Abraham's Four Seeds
But I Say Unto You
Chosen In Eternity
Christ, Lord and Lawgiver Over the Church
Grace
Limited Atonement
The New Birth
Our Sovereign God
The Sovereignty of God in Prayer
The Sovereignty of God in Providence
Tablets of Stone
Total Depravity
What is the Christian Faith?

THE BELIEVER'S SABBATH

John G. Reisinger

5317 Wye Creek Drive, Frederick, MD 21703-6938
Phone: 301-473-8781 or 800-376-4146   Fax: 301-473-5128
Website: www.soundofgracebooks.com
Email: info@soundofgracebooks.com

In this book, the author has placed certain words from Scriptural quotations in italics or bold print without individually marking each instance with such words as "italics mine." The reader should be aware, however, that these italics and bold print are not found in the original texts but are added by the author for reasons of emphasis and clarity.

THE BELIEVER'S SABBATH

Copyright © 2002 by John G. Reisinger
ISBN 1-928965-12-1
Requests for information should be addressed to:
New Covenant Media
5317 Wye Creek Drive
Frederick, MD 21703-6938

Scripture quotations marked (NIV) are taken from the HOLY BIBLE, NEW INTERNATIONAL VERSION® NIV® Copyright©1973, 1978, 1984 by International Bible Society. Used by permission. All rights reserved.

Scripture quotations marked "NKJV" are taken from the New King James Version. Copyright © 1982 by Thomas Nelson, Inc. Used by permission. All rights reserved.

All other Scripture quotations are taken from the King James Version.

All rights reserved. No part of this publication may be reproduced, stored in a retrieval system, or transmitted in any form or by any means—electronic, mechanical, photocopy, recording, or any other—except for brief quotations in printed reviews, without the prior permission of the publisher.

In the Epistle to the Philippians, the Apostle Paul issues one of the most amazing statements any apostle ever uttered.

> *Let this mind be in you which was also in Christ Jesus, who, being in the form of God, did not consider it robbery to be equal with God, but made Himself of no reputation, taking the form of a bondservant, and coming in the likeness of men. And being found in appearance as a man, He humbled Himself and became obedient to the point of death, even the death of the cross. Therefore God also has highly exalted Him and given Him the name which is above every name, that at the name of Jesus every knee should bow, of those in heaven, and of those on earth, and of those under the earth, and that every tongue should confess that Jesus Christ is Lord, to the glory of God the Father. (Phil. 2:5-11 NKJV)*

The concept presented in II Corinthians 8:9 helps us grasp a bit of this majesty.

> *For you know the grace of our Lord Jesus Christ, that though He was rich, yet for your sakes He became poor, that you through His poverty might become rich. (NKJV)*

How rich was our Lord before he laid it all aside to become a servant? He owned everything. He was the object of the worship of all creation. How poor did he become? He could say, "The foxes have holes to sleep in but the Son of Man hath nowhere to lay His head." And how poor were we sinners before he came and died for us? All we had that we could call our own was our sin and shame. And how rich did he make us by adopting us into his family? We become a joint heir with the Lord of Glory himself. What a text!

Philippians 2:5-11 speaks of Christ as God and as man. It describes both his humiliation and exaltation, both his deity and humanity. It emphasizes that his humiliation was a conscious act on his part. This passage helps us to learn something of the wonder of our Lord by realizing who he really is, both as God and man. We learn who he is by seeing what he has done.

We want to discuss the work that our Lord accomplished which earned him the rewarded Lordship spoken of in Philippians 2:5-11. The gospel is the story of how Christ "finished the work my Father gave me to do." Learning the gospel is learning about HIM and the work he came to do.

Notice how Paul describes both Christ and the gospel in his introduction to the Book of Romans.

> *Paul, a bondservant of Jesus Christ, called to be an apostle, separated to the gospel of God which He promised before through His prophets in the Holy Scriptures, concerning His Son Jesus Christ our Lord, who was born of the seed of David according to the flesh, and declared to be the Son of God with power according to the Spirit of holiness, by the resurrection from the dead. (Rom. 1:1-4 NKJV)*

This text is usually used to prove both the humanity and the deity of Christ; that he was both God and man. Verse three is taken to be referring to his humanity, *(born of the seed of David according to the flesh)* and verse four is understood as the resurrection, proving his deity *(declared to be the Son of God with power according to the Spirit of holiness, by the resurrection from the dead)*. I do not for a moment question either the absolute deity or perfect humanity of Christ. The Bible clearly teaches both of these things and we must protect them both. However, that is not the point Paul is seeking to demonstrate in this text. If Paul had wanted to emphasize our Lord's humanity, he would have said, "son of Mary", not "son of David".

We remember how carefully Isaiah stated both of these things: Isaiah 9:6a, *For unto us a **Child is born,** unto us a **Son is given.*** Isaiah speaks of Christ as both a child and as a son. Why use both words? As a child, he is *born*, and as a Son, he is *given*. There is a great difference between those two things. One term is speaking of his humanity and the other term describes his deity. This text clearly reveals one of Rome's most blatant errors. Mary is not the 'Mother of God' as Rome asserts. She is the mother of the humanity of our Lord, but not the mother of his deity. God has no mother. Mary did not give birth to God, but she did give birth to a real man. Jesus, like any other man, had a real mother even though he did not have a human father. He was born in the same manner as every other man, but he was not begotten as other men. His humanity has a beginning point in time; it is his incarnation and birth. Jesus, as 'son of God' was not born, but always existed as the second person of the Trinity. The 'son' was 'given' by the Father, and the 'giving' was giving up to death. This child was born for the express purpose of dying in the place of his people.

I would suggest to you the following:

"Born of the seed of David" in Romans 1:4 does not emphasize Christ's humanity, but rather his right to sit on David's throne and fulfill the covenant that God made with David to 'raise up a son to sit on the throne' and 'receive all authority.' A much better way to stress his humanity would be to refer to Christ as 'son of Mary' or simply, 'born of a virgin.' Romans 1:4 refers to the same governorship, or, Lordship, that Isaiah 9:6, 7 does *('the government shall be upon his shoulders')*. Jesus today, right now, sits on David's throne. He is Lord over God's new, redeemed creation right now.

Paul is not, in this text, saying that the resurrection proves that Christ is God. He is saying that Christ, **the man,** received a new and unique Lordship at the resurrection and ascension as a reward for finishing the work his Father had given him to do. This work began the moment that sin destroyed God's first finished work.

The key thoughts in the creative week in Genesis are **work - finished - satisfied - rest.** Those very same words also describe the new creation established by the finished work of our Lord. Christ was always Lord, as the second person of the Trinity, but he became Lord **as a man** in a new and redemptive sense at the resurrection and ascension. The 'man' Christ Jesus has earned the right to rule and reign in sovereign grace. He is the undisputed Lord over God's new creation. Our Lord's right, or authority, to forgive sins is not part of his inherent Godhead as a member of the Trinity; this authority was given to him by the Father as an earned reward for his redemptive work. He can legally and righteously forgive sins because he paid for those sins. He can forgive sins because he perfectly satisfied the Father's righteous demands. He was rewarded with both the title of 'Lord' and the authority to exercise Lordship over everything and everybody (John 17:1-3).

There is not nearly enough emphasis on recognizing the work of Christ as beginning immediately after the fall of Adam. The redemptive work of Christ did not begin with the incarnation. That was only the beginning of the last stage. To understand the 'work' of Christ for which he was rewarded as described in Philippians 2:5-11 we must go back and begin at Genesis 1:1. As we look at those majestic words, notice that four things are going to be repeated on each of the six days of God's creative work.

1. God will state his specific purpose for each creative day's work.
2. The words *it was so* will indicate that the specific work announced was accomplished that day.
3. With the words *it was good,* God will express his total satisfaction with the work he has done that day.
4. The phrase 'the morning and the evening' will show the beginning and the end of the particular day when each phase of work was done.

Note the words in bold print in the first day of creation.

> *In the beginning God created the heaven and the earth. And the earth was without form, and void; and darkness was upon the face of the deep. And the Spirit of God moved upon the face of the waters. And* **God said, Let there be light:** *and* **there was light.** *And* **God saw the light,** *that it* **was good:** *and God divided the light from the darkness. And God called the light Day, and the darkness he called Night. And the* **evening** *and the* **morning** *were the* **first day**. *(Gen. 1:1-5)*

We will see all four of these things occurring on each of the first six days. Genesis 1:1 *"In the beginning God created the heavens and the earth"* is the general statement of the whole creative process, and then follows the description of the six-day's work.

Genesis 1:3 states God's intention 'to create light.'

Verse 3 states that the announced job is done.

Verse 4 shows God expressing his satisfaction with the work he has just done.

Verse 5 tell us that it was the "morning and evening of the first day."

It is essential that we get these words - **work - finished - satisfaction** - into our mind. They tell the story of God's creative activity at the dawn of time. Notice also that the words *evening* and *morning* of the 'first day' identify the specific day with the specific work done on that day. We will come back to this last point.

Gen. 1:6-10 records the **firmament and the dry land** being created on the second day.

Gen. 1:11-13 records the creation of **grass, trees, and other vegetation** on the third day.

Gen. 1:14-19 records the **sun, moon and stars** being created on the fourth day.

Gen. 1:20-26 records the creation of the **land creatures, birds and fish** on the fifth day.

Gen. 1:26-31 records the **creation of man in God's image** on the sixth day.

The next section contains the concluding statement concerning God's creative work. So far, everything had been consistent and uniform on each of the six days. The only variation is God saying 'very good' instead of just 'good' on the sixth day. Each day there was the specific work described, the work finished, the expressed satisfaction, and the beginning and end of the given creative day.

Look now at Genesis 2:1. *"Thus the heavens and the earth were finished, and all the host of them."* The key word here is *finished*. This is not an announcement concerning the seventh day's intended work, for no work was either announced or done on the seventh day. This announces the end of the whole creating purpose and process. This takes us back to the summary statement in Genesis 1:1.

The next verse, 2:2, begins with the word *and*, so we must not isolate it from the preceding verses. It is essential that we look carefully at what these verses actually say as well as at what they do not say.

> *And on the seventh day God ended his work which he had made; and he rested on the seventh day from all his work which he had made. And God blessed the seventh day, and sanctified it: BECAUSE that in it he had rested from all his work which God created and made. (Gen. 2:2, 3)*

Let me list some clear facts drawn from these verses. These are facts regardless of what view we take on the Sabbath. There is a disagreement among Christians, including Reformed Christians, on the subject of the Sabbath, or Fourth Commandment. If Genesis 2:2, 3 teach that God gave Adam the Sabbath as a 'Creation Ordinance', then the Sabbath argument is over. That one thing, if proven, is more than sufficient to prove that the Sabbath is a moral, not ceremonial, commandment binding on all men in all ages and not just binding on Israel. What do the verses actually say and not say?

ONE: These verses do not say that God commanded Adam to treat the seventh day differently than the other six. God may have commanded Adam to keep the seventh day differently than the other six but there is not the slightest bit of evidence for that in these two verses. Actually, the verses contain no commandment to Adam of any kind. The text deals exclusively with God's actions.

TWO: There is no record in Scripture that (1) Adam ever kept the seventh day any differently than the other six, but (2) there is some evidence that Adam did not observe a Sabbath day of rest prior to sin entering the world. These two biblical facts ought to make us stop and think. Regrettably, many preachers and theologians simply ignore these facts and load all kinds of things into these verses that are not there.

THREE: The seventh day is not called a Sabbath nor is it designated a Sabbath of rest anywhere in the account given in Genesis 2:1-3. Read these verses carefully and the above facts are very clear.

FOUR: There is not a single instance recorded in Scripture of anyone keeping the seventh day as a Sabbath day of rest until Exodus 16 and the giving of the manna. Exodus 16:23 is the first mention of the Sabbath in Scripture.

> Then he said to them, "This is what the LORD has said: 'Tomorrow is a Sabbath rest, a holy Sabbath to the LORD. (Ex. 16:23 NKJV)

FIVE: These facts[1] mean we must deal with some clear biblical information:

We have no biblical record of anyone keeping the Sabbath prior to Exodus 16 when God first gave the Sabbath to Israel, and we cannot use something not recorded as proof of something we want to believe. The words recorded in the actual texts of Scripture are the only valid evidence in any biblical argument. There is a specific text of Scripture where the Holy Spirit explicitly informs us that God first made known the Sabbath commandment at Mt. Sinai. This is a fact beyond dispute. We cannot reject a clear statement of Scripture just because it does not fit our system. Nehemiah is very explicit concerning when the Sabbath was first given. We dare not make unwarranted assumptions from Genesis 2:2, 3 that are not stated in the text, especially when those statements clearly contradict another clear text of Scripture.

> You came **down on Mount Sinai;** you spoke to them from heaven. You gave them regulations and laws that are just and right, and decrees and commands that are good. You **made known to them your holy Sabbath** and gave them commands, decrees and laws through your servant Moses. (Neh. 9:13, 14 NIV)

Notice that the Sabbath is set off from the commands, decrees and laws. This is because the Sabbath was the most important of all the Ten Commandments, and its importance lay in the fact that the Sabbath was the sign of the old covenant.

---

[1] For a detailed argument that the seventh-day Sabbath was not given to Adam, but was first given to Israel in Exodus 16, see Bunyan's article on the Sabbath or my article, *John Bunyan and the Sabbath*.

Some people say that Israel already had the Sabbath but they had forgotten it and God was reminding them. 'Making something known' and 'reminding you of something you already know' are two different things.

The foregoing five facts do not prove that the Sabbath is not a moral law, nor do these facts in themselves prove that the Sabbath was not given to Adam at Creation. However, these biblical facts do clearly prove that you cannot use Genesis 2:1-3 as a proof text for believing the Sabbath was given to Adam at creation. If you want to believe that the Sabbath is a 'creation ordinance,' you must use textual evidence other than Genesis 2:1-3, and as far as I know there isn't any such textual evidence!

We dare not use an argument as proof when the argument is not found in Scripture, and likewise, we dare not reject clear facts that are stated in related texts of Scripture. When we ask the question, "Does the Bible teach anywhere that anyone prior to Exodus 16:23, including Adam in Genesis 2:1-3, observed a Sabbath day of rest?" the answer must be "No, there is no such record." When we then ask the question, "Does Scripture ever tell us clearly when the Sabbath commandment was first given?" we must answer, "Yes, Nehemiah 9:13, 14 specifically tells us that the Sabbath was first given at Sinai to the Nation of Israel."

Since there is no record of Sabbath observance prior to Exodus 16, and since Nehemiah 9:13,14 specifically states that the Sabbath was first given to Israel at Sinai, then exactly what is God saying in Genesis? What do those verses mean? Let's look carefully at what the statements in Genesis 2:1-3 do teach.

> *Thus the heavens and the earth were finished, and all the host of them. And on the seventh day God ended his work which he had made; and he rested on the seventh day from all his work which he had made. And God blessed the seventh day, and sanctified it: because that in it he had rested from all his work which God created and made. (Gen.2:1-3)*

First, we immediately see that there is no 'morning or evening' announced to end the seventh day. This day is obviously different from the other six. It is especially significant that the seventh day had no work done nor did it have an end. It is open ended. That seventh day might still be going on today if sin had not entered the world and marred God's 'good' and 'finished' created work. Regardless, it is essential to see exactly how totally different this seventh day is from the other six days.

Let's ask and answer some obvious questions:

First question: Why did God 'rest' on the seventh day? Was he tired? No, God can never get tired. God rested in the enjoyment of what he had created. He rested because his work was finished. He stopped creating because he had finished doing everything he had set out to do.

Note the word *because* in Genesis 2:3. God declared the seventh day as different from the other six simply because he had finished his creative work or purposes. He rested only because he was finished. We dare not read some kind of fatigue or weariness into this text or we grossly misrepresent God. God rested simply because he had completely accomplished everything that he had set out to do.

The word *rest* in the fourth commandment, given to Israel in Exodus 20, deals with physical rest from burdensome labor. The slave does not 'rest in his accomplishments', in fact he may hate the work that he has been forced to do. God was not forced to work in the first place and he surely did not stop because he was tired and needed rest. God's rest in Genesis 2:1, 2 cannot be equated with Israel's rest in the wilderness in Exodus 20. The Israelite rested from his work because he was physically exhausted. In no sense can we compare God resting in appreciation of his creative work in Genesis 2:1-3 to Israel resting after a week of toil and sweat as in Exodus 20.

The fourth commandment rest is set in the context of deliverance from bondage and slavery. The Israelites were making bricks and had to gather their own straw. Exodus says, "They cried to God because of their bondage." None of the circumstances surrounding the giving of the law at Sinai could in any way be applicable to either God or Adam in Genesis 2:1-3. Neither God nor Adam ever cried out for rest because they were worn out in fatigue.

The fourth commandment given to Israel at Sinai did at least two things.

One: The Sabbath constantly reminded Israel of the rest that Adam had lost in the Garden of Eden because of his sin. Every seventh day, the Israelite was forced to remember the awful consequences of Adam's rebellion to God. He could compare his present life of hard work, needed just to survive, with the life where everything needed was provided by God, without pain and labor on his own part. In other words, the Sabbath was a weekly, constant, visible reminder of the wages of sin.

Two: The Sabbath also gave Israel a promise and hope of a coming Redeemer who would restore the rest that had been lost in Eden. The Sabbath preached the gospel as clearly as any ceremony in the whole Old Testament! The Sabbath was a clear picture of Christ and the rest that he would give. The entire Old Testament Scriptures speak of a coming 'rest,' or 'Sabbath.'

Our Lord's words "Do this...in remembrance of me" in I Corinthians 11:25-27 are a deliberate contrast between the two signs of the two covenant Sabbaths or rests. You need only put a little stress on the word *this* and the contrast is obvious. The Sabbath reminded Israel of the first creation and of God the Creator and his just and holy demands written on Tablets of Stone. Our Lord told us to remember the Cross and the new creation he finished by his redeeming work. One remembrance sign reminds us of the 'just, good, and holy law,' and both our duty and inability to keep it. The new remembrance sign reminds us of a 'new and better covenant' that assures us that all of the terms of the old covenant were perfectly met in our Surety. The Sabbath pointed to our ceasing from our works and resting in the finished work of Christ. A Sabbath at creation could have done neither of these things since they would have been both unnecessary and impossible.

Second question: Why did this seventh day, unlike the other six, have no end?

Maybe it was because there was to be a continual and unbroken rest for both God and man. God would delight and rest in his perfect creation, and Adam would find true rest and joy in everything he did. All of Adam's work was nothing less than worshiping and appreciating God's character as revealed in his creation. Adam did not sweat and labor for six days and then rest and worship for one day. Everything Adam did was worship and brought him rest. The more he labored, the more he worshipped, and the more he worshipped, the more he rested. God would rest in approving joy in his creation, and man would rest in obedient worship as he tended the garden. It is only because sin entered into the world that both God's rest and man's rest were broken.

It is essential that we remember several things about the Garden of Eden. Let me list some things that are often overlooked.

Eden was a perfect creation just as Adam was a perfect creature.

Eden was the perfect creation especially designed for the perfect creature. There was no toil, no sweat, no fighting weeds and thistles, in that perfect creation. There were no shortages, no fears, and no unfulfilled longings. *The seventh day was the essence of Eden itself! Eden was a perfect Sabbath rest in God's goodness and fellowship.*

When God said, "It is very good," that statement included every biological and psychological need that Adam had. Every true need in our whole being is God-given. The garden was designed to satisfy every need Adam and Eve had in a way that would make them supremely satisfied and fulfilled, and also would supremely glorify God in every single thing they did. God's finished work really was *finished* with full provisions for all of man's needs.

Such a situation is not even close to the environment of Exodus 20 when the fourth commandment was given to Israel. There simply is no comparison. Once man sinned, he forever came into constant conflict with God, with himself, with Eve, and with a harsh, God-cursed environment just to stay alive. None of those things had anything to do with God resting after finishing his creative work.

Third question: Did Adam need a day of rest from his job of ruling over God's whole creation? Look again at Genesis 1:26-31.

> *And God said, Let us make man in our image, after our likeness: and let them have dominion over the fish of the sea, and over the fowl of the air, and over the cattle, and over all the earth, and over every creeping thing that creepeth upon the earth. So God created man in his own image, in the image of God created he him; male and female created he them. And God blessed them, and God said unto them, Be fruitful, and multiply, and replenish the earth, and subdue it: and have dominion over the fish of the sea, and over the fowl of the air, and over every living thing that moveth upon the earth. And God said, Behold, I have given you every herb bearing seed, which is upon the face of all the earth, and every tree, in the which is the fruit of a tree yielding seed; to you it shall be for meat. And to every beast of the earth, and to every fowl of the air, and to every thing that creepeth upon the earth, wherein there is life, I have given every green herb for meat: and it was so. And God saw every thing that he had made, and, behold, it was very good. And the evening and the morning were the sixth day.*

Was this a responsibility that brought such physical exhaustion that he needed a rest from his work? We know that Adam did not sweat before sin entered into the world. He never had sore muscles. Actually, there could have been no six and one division of time based on 'work' versus 'worship' or 'work' versus 'rest' in the Garden of Eden. There was no 'work' in Eden in the sense of 'work' in Exodus. There are no secular/religious categories in Adam's experience until sin enters the world.

There was no working against the elements because everything, including the ground and weather, was one hundred percent friendly to Adam. He never worked for a single meal in his whole existence in the garden. There was no 'earning by the sweat of your brow' in the perfect creation into which God put Adam. Everything Adam did was worship. Nothing he did could make him either need or want to stop his work. The more he worked, the more he worshipped, and the more he worshipped, the more he was filled with joy and rest in the presence of God.

Adam's work was his refreshment. Adam saw God in everything he did. Everything he did was a delightful experience of worship and praise to God, his friend and great benefactor. We can no more read the idea of resting because of being dead tired and worn out into Adam's pre-sin experience than we can read it into God's resting after completing his creation work. There could not have been a six and one day cycle in Eden anymore than there can be one in heaven. Are we going to work and toil by the sweat of our brow in heaven for six days and then have a day to rest from the burdensome toil? The idea is ridiculous! Will we have six days of work and then one day of worship? Nonsense. We will not have six days for ourselves and one day for God.

Read again the curse upon man and upon creation in Genesis Gen. 3:16-19.

> *Unto the woman he said, I will greatly multiply thy sorrow and thy conception; in sorrow thou shalt bring forth children; [The woman will feel pain for the first time while obeying the very commandment of God to bring forth children.] and thy desire shall be to thy husband, and he shall rule over thee. [The full co-worker status is now changed to one of headship.] And unto Adam he said, Because thou hast hearkened unto the voice of thy wife, and hast eaten of the tree, of which I commanded thee, saying, Thou shalt not eat of it: cursed is the ground for thy sake; in sorrow shalt thou eat of it all the days of thy life; Thorns also and thistles shall it bring forth to thee; and thou shalt eat the herb of the field; In the sweat of thy face shalt thou eat bread, [No more 'free lunch'] till thou return unto the ground; for out of it wast thou taken: for dust thou art, and unto dust shalt thou return.*

The ground is cursed because of Adam's sin. Think of Genesis 3:17 and 18 when you read Romans 8:18-24.

> *I consider that our present sufferings are not worth comparing with the glory that will be revealed in us. [Remember that not one of those sufferings or hardships was experienced in Eden before Adam fell. They are all a direct result of sin entering into the world and*

destroying both God's and Adam's rest.] The creation waits in eager expectation for the sons of God to be revealed. For the creation was subjected to frustration, [The very creation which God carefully created and then pronounced 'very good' and in which he could take pleasure and rest is now under his curse.] not by its own choice, [Unlike Adam, creation did not have a free will] but by the will of the one who subjected it, in hope that the creation itself will be liberated from its bondage to decay [Do you realize the import of this fact? The very creation in which God rested in satisfaction is now in bondage and decay and under his curse. The very creation that God pronounced "very good" is scheduled for the fire to be burned up!] and brought into the glorious freedom of the children of God. We know that the whole creation has been groaning as in the pains of childbirth right up to the present time. [Creation awaits liberation] Not only so, but we ourselves, who have the firstfruits of the Spirit, [the assurance of forgiveness and the witness of the Spirit] groan inwardly [as expressed in Romans 7] as we wait eagerly for our adoption as sons, the redemption of our bodies. For in this hope we were saved. But hope that is seen is no hope at all. Who hopes for what he already has? (NIV)

There was a Sabbath rest lost in Eden and an even greater Sabbath rest regained at Calvary! Remember what we said about the two great lessons. The old Sabbath, (1) reminded Israel of the rest that was lost in Eden, and (2) it gave them hope of a new Sabbath that would restore more than was lost in Eden. Neither of these things was either possible or necessary before the fall.

Fourth question: Does the Scripture clearly show that God immediately went back to work the very moment that sin came into the world? I believe it does and that it also gives a valuable key to understanding both the work and the rest of God. Remember the order of that first creative work of God in Genesis.

(1) Work announced.
(2) Work finished.
(3) Satisfaction with the work.
(4) Rest in the finished work.

Consider this: Genesis 3:15 is the *announcement* of God going back to work. The words from the cross, "It is finished," are the *declaration that the new work announced in Genesis 3:15 is now completed.* God is saying in the resurrection and ascension, "It is very good. I am perfectly satisfied with my Son's work of a new creation." Our Lord 'sitting down at the right hand of God' signifies his resting from his finished work.

Actually, the whole 'work my Father gave me' motif in the New Testament Scriptures as applied to the ministry of our Lord would have no meaning without putting it into the context of Genesis 2:1-3. We will examine this point shortly.

Let's review what we have stated thus far:
1) There is no recorded command given to Adam in Genesis to keep a Sabbath day.
2) There is not a single example given in Scripture of a Sabbath being kept by anyone, including Adam, until Exodus 16:23.
3) We are told in Nehemiah 9:13, 14 that the Sabbath was first given to Israel at Sinai.
4) The obvious omission of the phrase 'the morning and evening' in Genesis 2:2, 3 thus leaving the seventh day open-ended, shows that the seventh day could still be going on if sin had not entered into the world and marred God's good and finished creative work.

The second thing we should notice in Genesis 2:2, 3 is the explicit language used to describe God's creative activity. Notice how four words tell the whole story.

1. The first word is *work*.
2. The second word is *finished*.
3. The third word is *good*.
4. The fourth word is *rested*.

God followed the identical pattern in his new creation.
1) He announced his intention to send his Son to remedy the tragedy of the fall.
2) God finished his planned work of redemption and re-creation at the cross.

3) God was very pleased with the work accomplished by his Son.
4) God rested in what he had accomplished through the work of his Son.

What comes into your mind as you repeat the words **work - finished - satisfied – rest** found in Genesis? I am sure we can easily connect those words to the New Creation of God wrought by our blessed Redeemer. We can hear the words "It is finished" coming from the cross as we read Genesis 2:1-3. This is especially true as we keep remembering our Lord's emphasis that he was 'doing the work my Father gave me to do.' When we see him who cried out, "It is finished," raised from the dead and ascending to glory, we hear the Father saying, "I am perfectly satisfied with my Son's work."

When we read the gospel expressed in passages like Matthew 11:28-30, '. . . *come unto me all ye that labor and are heavy laden and I will give you rest,*' or 'I will **sabbath** your souls,' we find God inviting us to enter his rest with him through our Lord Jesus Christ.

The third thing we must remember and emphasize is that the moment sin entered into God's perfect creation and defaced it, God, in accordance with his holiness and justice, cursed both the creation and the man who had sinned and ruined that creation.

The very creation in which God rested and said was very good is now cursed by God, forsaken, and turned over to vanity and corruption (Rom. 8:19-22). The man created in the very image of God has now become the enemy of God (Eph. 2:3; Rom. 5). Both the perfect created earth and the perfect created man are cursed by God and are under his wrath.

The fourth thing to realize and emphasize is that God immediately went back to work the moment Adam sinned.

It is this point that is not at all emphasized by most theologians. The history of redemption, or of the new creation, began to be worked out in that first promise of the seed of the woman who would undo what Adam's sin had done. We know this work was planned in eternity (Rev. 13:8) and the first step in carrying it out was put into effect in Genesis 3:15.

I ask again, what is Genesis 3:15 but *the announcement that God has gone back to work?* Notice how carefully the working out of the new creation follows the pattern of the old creation. There is:

1) the announcement of the intended work—the seed of the woman is going to crush the serpent's head;
2) the work is perfectly accomplished or completed when Christ defeats Satan at the cross;
3) God expresses his satisfaction with the finished work by raising our Lord from the dead, and seating him at his right hand with all power; and
4) *God forever rests in his new created work.*

God gave a promise that a Last Adam would come into the world and accomplish a work that could never again be affected by sin or anything else. This new creation would bring more honor and glory to God than ten thousand Gardens of Eden. This would be a work in which God could rest in delight for all eternity. This would be the true eternal Sabbath!

Yes, God went back to work when sin destroyed his first creation and he did not quit until he finished the work of the new creation at the cross.

The 'rest' resulting from that gracious and powerful work accomplished by Christ has nothing to do with a twenty-four hour day. It brings a day of rest that is truly without end and not just twenty-four hours long. It brings in 'that day' and 'that rest' which the Old Testament kept looking forward to and the New Testament says has finally dawned. 'This is the Day the Lord hath made' has nothing to do with either Saturday or Sunday. That is not a twenty-four hour Sabbath day but an eternal Sabbath rest that truly has no end.

Notice that God's new work is a totally new creation. It is not a patch-up of the old creation. The old was cursed and destined for a fiery destruction including Adam's return to the dust from which he was made. A whole new creation with a new race of redeemed men and women with a new head was to be created on the foundation of the coming Redeemer's glorious work. The fruit of this work is in the mind of the writer of Hebrews when he speaks of 'many sons' and 'my brethren' being led to glory.

This second great work of God was forever finished at the cross. Those memorable words 'it is finished' refer to this second work of God. God saw how good that work was, and he was perfectly satisfied. The clear proof of just how satisfied God was with that great work is proven in the resurrection, ascension, and exaltation of the one who performed that great work.

The Father not only raised his Son from the grave, he also exalted him to the position of highest power and authority. After finishing the work, our Lord was raised from the dead. He then ascended into heaven, into the most holy place itself. And what did he do? **HE SAT DOWN! HE RESTED!**

Why did he sit down and rest? For the same reason the Father rested in Genesis 2:1-3. He sat down and rested because he was **completely finished with his work of re-creation.** He entered into the eternal Sabbath Day of rest!

I love that passage in Hebrews 1:3, "Who being the brightness of his glory, and the express image of his person, and upholding all things by the word of his power, when he had by himself purged our sins, **sat down on the right hand of the Majesty on high.**"

HE SAT DOWN! Why did he sit down? Well, it was not because he was tired! I keep repeating this because it is so important. He sat down for the same reason his Father rested after finishing the first creation. He sat down because his work was done and it was done forever!

Where did he sit down? At the right hand of God the Father Almighty! Hebrews 10:5-12 illustrates this same point:

> *Wherefore when he cometh into the world, [Why did he come into the world? He came to do a job that his Father had given him to do!] he saith, Sacrifice and offering thou wouldest not, but a body hast*

thou prepared me: [He needed a human sinless body in order to do the work he had been given to do. That body was prepared by the Holy Spirit in Mary's womb was his perfect humanity. He must take on humanity if he is to redeem humanity. This is why the New Testament Scriptures emphasize Christ's 'body.' This stresses his sinless humanity.] In burnt offerings and sacrifices for sin thou hast had no pleasure. Then said I, Lo, I come (in the volume of the book it is written of me,) [all the Old Testament Scriptures are about Christ coming as the fulfillment of Genesis 3:15] to do thy will, O God. [God's will for him was to die on the cross to work out a perfect redemption. That was the foreordained work the Son agreed to in eternity.] Above when he said, Sacrifice and offering and burnt offerings and offering for sin thou wouldest not, neither hadst pleasure therein; which are offered by the law; Then said he, Lo, I come to do thy will, O God. He taketh away the first [the first expression of his will, or the first covenant], that he may establish the second. [This new and everlasting covenant will need no additions, and will never be changed. It is a sure and completed covenant.] By the which will we are sanctified through the offering of the body of Jesus Christ once for all. [The Father's expressed will is seen at Calvary where our Lord's perfect humanity was laid on the altar of his absolute deity and a perfect work of atonement was completed.] And every priest standeth daily ministering and offering oftentimes the same sacrifices, which can never take away sins: [Those priests worked and worked without ever sitting down. Their work was never complete and all their work put together could never atone for one single sin.] But this man, [or priest] after he had offered one sacrifice for sins for ever, sat down on the right hand of God;

Why did our Lord sit down and rest? I keep repeating it! It was for the same reason God the Father rested in Genesis 2:3. He sat down and rested because the planned and announced work was finished. We must get this into our minds and hearts! Our Lord sat down and rested both *from* and *in* his great work! Why did he sit down? His work was done. He had completed the job his Father had given him to do! He had brought in 'that day,' the true Sabbath Day that the entire Old Testament Scriptures anticipated. God was just as satisfied with the second creation as he was with the first creation because they were both his sovereign and exclusive work, and both works were completed exactly as he had planned them. That is why God could rest in both of these works.

One of the great differences in the two works is that sin can never in any way mar this final, once for all, great work! God has been resting in the Redeemer's great work ever since it was finished and he graciously calls us to enter into that rest with him (Heb. 4:9-11; Matt. 11:28-30). I think it is fair to say that the whole of the New Testament Scriptures are built around God's new work and the rest that it secures. I do not think we can understand the 'work of God' referred to in the following verses as anything other than the work of redemption that God began the very day he cursed the first creation that was no longer a source of rest to him. What else could the following text be talking about?

> *I have glorified thee on the earth: I have **finished the work** which thou gavest me to do." (John 17:4)*

What work is our Lord talking about? Of course, we know, as already mentioned, the plan for this work was laid in eternity (Rev. 13:8). However, the implementing and carrying out of that foreordained work in time began in Genesis the moment sin entered and destroyed that first creation of God.

Let me list just a few other texts that clearly teach this same truth. The reader can easily work out the implications.

- John 4:34; Jesus saith unto them, My meat is to do the will of him that sent me, and to **finish his work.**
- John 5:36; But I have greater witness than that of John: for **the works which the Father hath given me to finish,** the same works that I do, bear witness of me, that the Father hath sent me.
- John 5:17; But Jesus answered them, My Father **worketh hitherto, and I work.**
- John 19:30; When Jesus therefore had received the vinegar, he said, **It is finished:** and he bowed his head, and gave up the ghost.
- John 9:4; I must **work the works of him that sent me,** while it is day: the night cometh, when no man can work.

> Eph. 2:10; For we are **his workmanship,** created in Christ Jesus unto good works, which God hath before ordained that we should walk in them.

Review the four words that summarize that first creative week in Genesis chapter 1: *Work – finished – good – rested,* and notice how all of the above texts speak of Christ 'working.' What specific work of Christ are they talking about? Most theologians say this refers to our Lord working in providence. This is true, but it is not the meaning of these texts. When did God begin the work referred to in these texts? How do the answers to these questions fit into God 'ceasing to work and resting' in Genesis 2:1-3 and how we 'cease from our work' (Rom. 4:4, 5) when we rest in the cross? I think the answers to all of these questions are very clear.

The first creative work of God provided him a place where he could rest and enjoy the fruit of his labor. The second creative work does the same thing. However, this second work and rest provides a place of eternal rest that cannot be destroyed.

Applications:

Nearly all Sabbatarian writers judge the motives of those who disagree with them. They portray themselves as protectors of the glory of God by 'defending his holy law' against its enemies. They label any and all who disagree with them as 'antinomians' who hate God's law, simply because those who disagree insist that the fourth commandment is a ceremonial and not a moral law. These accusations need to be discussed in more detail, but for now, let me say that this booklet alone should demonstrate the motives in our hearts. We believe that the glory of our great Redeemer's work of redemption in providing a place of everlasting rest is often overshadowed when a twenty-four hour 'holy day' given to Israel gets more attention than the 'eternal holy day' of rest provided by Christ.

When the fulfillment of the twenty-four hour Sabbath day becomes nothing more than the changing of that day from Saturday to Sunday, then the true rest of Hebrews 4 is lost in the shuffle. *When the first creation of God is given more prominence than his second great work, it is the amazing power and grace of*

God itself that is easily eclipsed. When the old legal covenant, which was codified in nothing less than the Ten Commandments (Ex. 34:27-29; Deut. 9:9-11), is given more attention, and in some instances even more authority over the conscience of a child of God, than the new covenant of grace in the atoning blood of Christ (Heb. 8:6-8, Gal. 4:21-31; I Cor. 11:23-26), then the glory of Christ's redemptive work is diminished in direct proportion.

When the memorial sign, the Sabbath (Ex. 31:12-18), of the old legal covenant, becomes more important in a system of theology than the memorial sign, the Lord's Supper (I Cor. 11:23-25), of the New Covenant, then the atoning work of Christ can easily get lost in the shadows.

Our view of the Sabbath as the true goal of Christ's redeeming work grows out of our appreciation of him performing to perfection 'the work my Father gave me to do.' Anything that in any way hinders a believer from seeing Jesus Christ our Lord as the true and final fulfillment of everything the Sabbath pointed to should cause us to be concerned.

I do not question the motives of those who disagree with me on the Sabbath. I have said, and say again, many Sabbatarians love God just as much as I do. They sincerely hold their beliefs because they are convinced that is what the Scriptures teach. They are honestly concerned for the glory of God. I believe they are mistaken in their understanding of Scriptures concerning law and grace. I think they have allowed their theology to cloud their thinking. However, I in no way question their Christian integrity or love of Christ.

Can we not disagree with each other without judging motives? Can we not have an open discussion of the Word of God itself without anyone hiding behind a confession of faith? I challenge anyone to find a single antinomian statement in anything I have published. Challenging the system known as Covenant Theology does not automatically make one an antinomian!

All that we ask is that those who disagree with us demonstrate from Scripture where we are wrong. Show us from Genesis 2:1-3 that those texts teach the Sabbath is a 'Creation Ordinance'. Show us where our understanding of Nehemiah 9:13, 14 and the first giving of the Sabbath is wrong. Give us the texts of Scripture that prove there were people who kept the Sabbath prior to Exodus 16:23. We love both God and his law as much as the Sabbatarian. We merely differ on what that law really says and means.

One last point concerns the Sabbath and the gospel in the Old Testament. I mentioned earlier that the Sabbath was a great example of gospel preaching in the Old Testament Scriptures. Let me explain what I mean.

First of all, the essence of 'keeping the Sabbath holy' was refraining from physical work. Doing physical work was the only way you could break the Sabbath in Israel. There was no 'going to church' or any other prescribed worship connected with the Sabbath. This was clear from the first institution of the Sabbath in Exodus 16. Look at the first mention of the Sabbath in Scripture.

> *And it came to pass, that on the sixth day they gathered twice as much bread, two omers for one man: and all the rulers of the congregation came and told Moses. And he said unto them, This is that which the LORD hath said, Tomorrow is the rest of the holy sabbath unto the LORD: bake that which ye will bake to day, and seethe that ye will seethe; and that which remaineth over lay up for you to be kept until the morning. And they laid it up till the morning, as Moses bade: and it did not stink, neither was there any worm therein. And Moses said, Eat that today; for today is a sabbath unto the LORD: today ye shall not find it in the field. Six days ye shall gather it; but on the seventh day, which is the sabbath, in it there shall be none. And it came to pass, that there went out some of the people on the seventh day for to gather, and they found none. And the LORD said unto Moses, How long refuse ye to keep my commandments and my laws? See, for that the LORD hath given you the sabbath, therefore he giveth you on the sixth day the bread of two days; abide ye every man in his place, let no man go out of his place on the seventh day. So the people rested on the seventh day. (Ex. 16:22-30)*

Verse 29 says that God 'gave you the Sabbath.' You don't 'give something' to someone who already has it. They were to gather enough manna on the sixth day for two days and God promised it would not, as was the case on any other day, spoil. They could trust God that the manna would keep. They were to totally rest on the seventh day. They were not even allowed to walk out and gather the manna.

Later, when the Sabbath is given as the sign of the covenant, it became crystal clear that the only way to break the Sabbath was physical work. Exodus 31:14-15 is quite explicit.

> *Ye shall keep the sabbath therefore; for it is holy unto you: every one that defileth it shall surely be put to death: for whosoever doeth any work therein, that soul shall be cut off from among his people. Six days may work be done; but in the seventh is the sabbath of rest, holy to the LORD: whosoever doeth any work in the sabbath day, he shall surely be put to death.*

They are commanded in verse 14 to 'not defile the Sabbath,' and Moses immediately equates 'defiling the Sabbath' with doing any physical work. Both verses state that any form of physical work would result in death. There is a constant refrain of "Do not work upon pain of death." Don't even lift a finger to pick up sticks. "Cease from your work and rest." God told them they were to gather two days supply on the sixth day. "Trust me, it will not spoil" as it would on any other day.

As you read all the Sabbath references, you keep hearing, "Cease from your work, and trust me". The message is 'faith, not works.' You can hear the echoes of Romans 4:4, 5 crying out, "To him that worketh not but believeth . . ." The Sabbath pushed a man away from works to the rest of faith. The Sabbath preached the gospel of rest.

The yearly Sabbath also preached the gospel.

The twenty-fifth chapter of Leviticus describes the yearly Sabbath. Just as there was a weekly Sabbath (as well as many other Sabbaths, since most of the holy days were Sabbaths regardless of which day they fell on), there was a seventh year Sabbath. Just as the weekly Sabbath commanded 'no work' so the seventh year Sabbath commanded no work during the entire year. They could do no physical work at all for one whole year. They were not allowed to plow, cultivate or harvest for a whole year. They could eat from the land and the grapevines, but the poor and the stranger could do likewise. Verses 25-27 are instructive.

> You may ask, "What will we eat in the seventh year if we do not plant or harvest our crops?" I will send you such a blessing in the sixth year that the land will yield enough for three years. While you plant during the eighth year, you will eat from the old crop and will continue to eat from it until the harvest of the ninth year comes in. (Lev 25:20-22 NIV)

Again God was teaching, "You do not live by your works but by my grace. Trust me; allow the land to lie idle, I will give you all you need." Like the weekly Sabbath, the seventh year Sabbath also pushed the Israelite from works to faith. It preached the gospel. It forced him to faith as opposed to living by his own work.

The greatest of all Sabbaths was every fifty years. Just as six days were followed by a Sabbath day of rest, and six years were followed by a Sabbath year of rest, the seventh Sabbath year was followed by the Year of Jubilee. All debts and mortgages of every kind were canceled. Everyone returned to the original land that was given to his fathers.

You can imagine an Israelite who was in debt, with the family farm mortgaged. He would rise early on the morning of Jubilee and eagerly wait to hear the trumpet of the ram's horn and the announcement that 'Jubilee had come'. That is exactly what our Lord did in Luke 4:19 when he said he came to proclaim the 'acceptable year of the Lord,' or 'the year of the Lord's favor.' He was putting the gospel trumpet to his lips and saying, 'Jubilee has come; the Lord's great Sabbath day has dawned.' We have regained in Christ far more than we lost in Eden. Every debt we owe is paid and we are totally free. We live in the year of Jubilee. We have entered into the true Sabbath rest in Christ.

Some years ago, a friend preached a sermon from Hebrews 4 and covered some of the things I just mentioned. One woman who heard it said, "That is the first sermon I ever heard on the Sabbath that made me happy." That was because it was the first biblical sermon she had ever heard on the Sabbath. She had heard many sermons on 'Sabbath dos and don'ts, but she had never heard a Christ-centered sermon on the Sabbath having been forever fulfilled. Let me close with three clear statements:

One: If a sermon on the Sabbath of God does not make you want to shout for joy, then the preacher did not preach about God's true Sabbath.

Two: If you did not get a clear, close up view of Christ and his saving benefits that have been given to you by his 'work,' then you did not hear a biblical sermon on the Sabbath rest of God.

Three: If your Sabbath theology has never gotten you past the seventh day of the week to the 'Day of Salvation,' nor gotten you out of Exodus 20 to stand under the cross, to see the resurrection and gaze upon the ascended Christ, then you do not correctly understand the Sabbath. Christ is himself the Sabbath, and biblical Sabbath preaching always leads to the cross and the joy of assurance of salvation.